I0149120

Tamar's Scars

Tamar's Scars

CHRISTIAN REFLECTIONS ON THE EMOTIONAL, RELATIONAL, AND SPIRITUAL SCARS LEFT BY SEXUAL ABUSE

RENIKKO BIVENS

Graced
In Write

Copyright © 2023 by Renikko Bivens

ISBN 978-1-960658-01-2 Paperback

ISBN 978-1-960658-03-6 DIGITAL

All rights reserved.

No part of this book may be reproduced in any form or by any electronic or mechanical means, including information storage and retrieval systems, without written permission from the author, except for the use of brief quotations in a book review.

Unless otherwise indicated, all Scripture quotations are taken from the *New King James Version of the* Bible.

Disclaimer:

This book is designed to provide information, from a religious perspective, that may be controversial for some readers. Therefore, the advice and revelations presented may not be suitable for everyone. This work is sold with the understanding that neither the author nor the publisher is held responsible for any losses or damages that occur as a result of the information provided.

This book contains a collection of true stories from my personal experiences. To protect the privacy and identities of the individuals involved, I have changed names and, in some cases, employed dramatic storytelling techniques. The purpose of these alterations is to prevent any specific person from being identified or harmed by the content of this book.

Graced to Write LLC
The Spirit-Led Pen
P.O. Box 5813,
Sandersville, GA 31082
thespiritledpen.com

I want to thank Pastor Diane Spikes and Pastor Mia Roberson for inspiring me to complete this project. Your unwavering support, guidance, and prayers have been instrumental in its creation.

I want to express my gratitude to Pastor Diane. Thank you for being a compassionate listener, wise advisor, and fervent prayer warrior. Your dedication and support have propelled this project forward.

I want to express my gratitude to Pastor Mia. Thank you for your intercession. Your faith and commitment to uplifting others have infused this endeavor with inspiration and strength.

- Nikko

Table of Contents

Introduction to Tamar's Scars:

CONCEIVING TAMAR'S SCARS

Triggers are those things that cause your mind and emotions to be flooded with memories. They can evoke both horrible and beautiful nostalgic memories. A trigger can occur in various forms such as a word, touch, smell, sound, place, and so on. Triggers are incredibly powerful, capable of causing you to relive events, regardless of how much time has passed since they occurred. The best way that people have been taught to deal with negative triggers is to avoid them.

Avoiding triggers may work for the anticipated triggering event, but nothing prepares you for the unexpected, unpredictable, and unrehearsed triggers. The idea for Tamar's Scars was conceived after one of these triggering events.

If you recall, in Battles and Trials, I spoke about the "monster." Of the entire book, I have received more questions about the monster than anything else. This is because I did not delve deeply into the experience, but only provided a mere allusion. It was purposely written that way because it was an area in my life that hadn't healed enough for me to fully explore and discuss. My soul still required significant healing.

However, in February 2022, I was faced with reality. While speaking with a church member after service, they said something that sent me back over 20 years to that unhealed place. It was one of those triggers that hit me, blindsided me, and caught me off guard. I remember experiencing intense pain, my anxiety taking over, and coming close to having a panic attack.

The ride home from church was quiet, but my mind was filled with a whirlwind of thoughts and emotions. There was a lot of hypocrisy in the situation because, as a counselor and a professional, I help other people sort through their issues. I am seen as a master encourager and motivator in the lives of others, but I was an unhealed soul in my own life. That's hypocrisy.

As a black woman, I've always been aware of the expectations placed on me and how I should present myself to the world. I grew up hearing other black women say that in this world, I was born with two strikes against me. 1. I am a woman and 2. I was black, so that meant I had to be even better, even greater, just to receive the same recognition. So, I have learned to be strong, independent, educated, and hardworking. Even when I am hurting, I have learned to conceal my own scars and wounds because they are seen as signs of weakness. In my world, weakness was synonymous with failure, and there was no room for failure.

Tamar's Scars has compelled me to reflect on my own past and the narratives of sexual trauma shared by numerous women and men (yes, men). It is striking how we all share similar experiences despite our diverse backgrounds. We felt like we could manage on our own, taking control of our situation, without realizing how our failure to truly heal was robbing us not only of life but also of the life that God had destined for us.

It took some time, but I finally began to recognize that

what I experienced at church was not coincidental. This time, the effects of the trigger didn't go away. They stayed and lingered for so long until I finally came to the understanding that this was a place that God was opening up for me to heal. (Physician, heal thyself).

The very first thing I did was pray about it. Then, I spoke to my pastor about my feelings, my heart, my indifferences, and my frustrations. I finally reached a point where I was able to fully disclose what happened to me. I was sick and nervous when I told her. I almost felt like I was being exposed as a fraud.

My pastors had instilled trust in me to conduct Sunday services and teach. I love the Bible, studying it, and teaching it. However, I used to feel that my trauma would disqualify me or make me ineligible to serve God. I felt like an imposter. Teaching God's word with this profound spiritual impact that has never fully healed.

After I told her what I'd experienced in my past, I remember, my pastor taking a long pause. Then she said, "We will get through this." Her choice of words was God's confirmation in my situation. As a counselor, I have allied with and advocated for many people, but I have never experienced having someone to ally with and advocate for me. I remember feeling safe and relieved; a sense of deliverance and healing began to take place.

She did ask me if she could speak with another person (another Pastor that I trust) and have them pray in agreement for my situation. The last thing she told me was that she didn't know how long the process would be. However, she advised me not to rush it and to seek professional counseling if God led me to do so (again).

That is the message I want readers to take away from Tamar's Scars. It's okay to get help. It's okay to need help. It doesn't say anything negative about you. If you take nothing else from Tamar's Scars, if God has allowed you to come across this book, it may serve as the catalyst you need to inspire you to seek deliverance and healing. It's not just my story in these pages, but a collection of stories, so you'll know that you're not alone and that healing is possible.

Be blessed, and let the journey begin.

Who is Tamar?

UNDERSTANDING THE PAIN AND STRUGGLES OF A SURVIVOR

Let's explore the story of Tamar, a woman who faced a great deal of grief and adversity. Tamar was the daughter of King David and had a half-brother named Amnon. Amnon had developed romantic feelings for her because he found her attractive.

In a scheme to be alone with Tamar, Amnon pretended to be sick and asked their father to send Tamar to take care of him. King David agreed and sent Tamar to Amnon's house. Once they were alone, Amnon revealed his true intentions. He wanted more than just her care; he wanted to be intimate with her.

Tamar pleaded with Amnon, begging him not to violate her. But he didn't care about her pleas and was determined to have his way with her. Using his strength to overpower Tamar, he violated her in the most horrifying manner.

After the assault, Amnon's feelings for Tamar instantly turned to hatred. Can you imagine the nerve of Amnon to despise Tamar after he was the one who violated her? At this moment, Amnon exhibits the typical mindset of many abusers. They exploit people to fulfill a need and then discard them once that need has been met. Leaving the victim feeling used, worthless, and insignificant.

Amnon ordered his servants to throw her out and locked the door behind her. Tamar was humiliated and left Amnon's house in tears.

When Tamar arrived home, she shared what had happened to her with her brother, Absalom. Absalom was furious and he wanted justice for his sister. Unfortunately, after King David became aware of what had happened, he felt sorrowful but did not take any action to address the issue with Amnon. Instead, King David prioritized his son's reputation and their relationship over seeking justice for his daughter. It was a heartbreaking realization for her. Scripture says that Tamar would remain isolated and desolate in her brother Absalom's house (2 Samuel 13:20).

If you want to read the full account of Tamar and Amnon, you can find it in 2 Samuel 13. Let's examine Tamar's story.

Tamar's experience was life-altering. During this period in history, a woman who was still a virgin was highly regarded, and although not being a virgin did not guarantee that she would never marry, it significantly reduced her chances of finding a husband. Not being married meant she would have no one to care for her during a time when men were primarily responsible for taking care of the needs of the home.

So, not only did Amnon steal her innocence, but he also stole her future. Tamar had to bear the burden and scars of what he did to her for the rest of her life.

And you know what? While the spirit of Amnon can be seen in today's abusers, the spirit and mindset of Tamar can also be seen in those who have experienced abuse. Many of us carry or have carried similar burdens throughout our lives. We have borne scars and wounds from our own experiences. The isolation and desolation that Tamar experienced have become a harsh reality for some. Whether expressed naturally, spiritually, or both, these unhealed scars have the power to control and keep people stuck, much like Tamar.

Healing requires us to confront our pain and face it head-on.

Some of the worst advice I ever received was that there are certain things so terrible that we should keep them to ourselves and carry them to our graves. I used to believe that suppressing my problems and avoiding discussing my pain was the solution to progressing in life. But I've come to realize that healing doesn't come from hiding. It comes from actively engaging in the healing process.

As believers, we sometimes expect instant healing or deliverance from God. While I believe He can perform miraculous acts, it is important to recognize that healing often requires a journey. We have to be realistic and open about our struggles, trusting that God will be with us every step of the way.

> "Reproach has broken my heart, and I am filled with heaviness. I searched for someone to show pity, but there was no one. I looked for comforters, but I found none." - Psalm 69:20 NKJV

Psalm 69 is a song written by King David. This verse captures the raw emotions and profound loneliness that I'm certain Tamar and other survivors can empathize with. It expresses our desire to be understood and cared for, for someone to notice our suffering and provide comfort. When

Tamar's world came crashing down around her, she sought comfort and justice, but found no one to offer the help and understanding she desperately needed.

But even in this hopeless place, there is a glimmer of hope for us. Healing and restoration are possible, even when they seem unattainable. This is a lesson we can learn from Tamar's experience. We can't allow ourselves to become disheartened or give in to the idea that we're alone and that no one understands. Instead, we can place our faith in the unwavering assurance that God will always be with us.

As King David laments the absence of comforters, we can find solace in the knowledge that God is the ultimate provider of comfort and compassion. God is trustworthy and constant, even when we feel like there is no one else to turn to. He is aware of our suffering, responsive to our prayers, and willing to be our refuge.

Part One

~~~

EMOTIONAL EFFECTS

What are Emotional Effects?

Emotions are innate, meaning that we are born with them. As babies, no one has to teach us to smile or laugh when we're happy, or to cry when we're hurting or in need, or to be angry at a perceived injustice. What we feel and how we interpret our emotions are what shape our actions, as they serve as an expression of our inner feelings.

As we go through life, things happen and they affect us, both positively and negatively. Those negative experiences have the tendency to change how we interpret and process situations, which leads to our expressions or behaviors also being affected.

I remember my sophomore year in college when I took Sociology 101. My professor had worked and researched the foster care system in Georgia. She was very passionate about foster children. She brought in a training video about the foster care system in Georgia. This video chronicled the story of a little girl who was about 9 years old.

It was hard for them to find a placement for her, and she spent her time bouncing from group home to group home. If

I can recall correctly, she had been to about 16 group homes within a year's time.

She came from a home where she had been neglected and molested for many years before she was finally taken away from her parents. Neglect and molestation were all she knew, so she learned to equate that with love and affection. So, when she got into the foster care system, she thought she was showing love because she liked the other kids and did to them what was done to her. However, due to never experiencing love in the proper way, she did not understand that her actions were inappropriate. So, people looked at her as a trouble-maker, vile, and predatory child. But she felt victimized and alone because, despite her love for people and her attempts to express it, she didn't realize that what she considered love was actually causing harm.

She eventually aged out of the foster care system.

After the video, you could hear a pin drop in the class-room. Most people's situations aren't as severe as hers, but trauma victims do experience emotional imbalances when they are not healed.

Misinterpreting love and misunderstanding its true essence, including the ability to feel, give, and express love. How often do we hear about women being in abusive relation-ships, yet still remaining in love with their abusers? They make excuses for their abusers, convinced that their abusers love them in return. Stockholm syndrome is a concept for a reason; trauma is powerful enough to manipulate our emotions into believing lies, even if the lie is about ourselves.

The conversation on the emotional effects of sexual trauma can take many different directions, but for simplicity's sake, we will focus on how it affects us individually and our sense of self.

I must warn you, this is not your typical Christian book. There is only so much that can be done to make this topic appealing and easy to understand. Honestly, there is no simple way to present this topic. So, there will be stories and a rawness that many are not prepared for. However, the goal is for believers who have dealt with these issues to finally realize that they are not alone. They will see that God still has a need and purpose for their lives and that it's time to embrace deliverance, healing, and the fullness of God.

For I will restore health to you And heal you of your wounds,' says the Lord, 'Because they called you an outcast *saying:* "This *is* Zion; No one seeks her." ' - Jeremiah 30:17 NKJV

Battling Fear in Our Minds

~~~

18-year-old Zara found herself on an 800-mile bus journey because she was unable to afford a plane ticket. Whenever possible, she tried to sit close to other female passengers for safety. Hours into the trip, fatigue overcame her, and she drifted into sleep.

Suddenly, she awoke to an unsettling sensation, someone touching and caressing her inappropriately. Her eyes opened to discover that the woman passenger that was once seated beside her was gone, and a man had taken her place. Panic surged as he fidgeted and rummaged through his coat.

Instinctively, Zara opened her mouth to scream, but her voice was silenced by a chilling click and the graze of a sharp object against her side. Looking down, she saw a gleaming silver knife embedded in her flesh. "Shhh, be quiet," the man cautioned her.

In silent agony, Zara endured until the next stop. As soon as the bus came to a halt, the assailant swiftly vanished into the bustling crowd, leaving her alone with the weight of the encounter. The incident shattered her sense of security and altered her perspective on the world.

That incident resulted in fear consuming her, and she became reluctant to venture beyond the safety of her home. Twenty years later, Zara had never left her city again. Family stopped inviting her on family trips, friends stopped inviting her on getaways because they knew she would say "no".

When asked why she never liked to go anywhere, Zara never had an answer. She'd lived this way for so long, that the bus incident was a distant memory. She didn't recognize how that one incident had changed her life and was still affecting her.

Before the triggering event at the church that I mentioned in the introduction, I often wondered why I was always so fearful and anxious. The Bible says that God has not given us a spirit of fear (2 Timothy 1:7). If He didn't give it to us, why was it so prevalent in my life?

According to psychology, trauma can have significant effects on the structure, function, and connections of the brain. These changes are not easily reversed, and it is not possible to simply "mind over matter" the functional and structural alterations in the brain. While psychology has provided a comprehensive explanation of the natural effects of trauma on the brain, we often overlook and neglect to discuss the spiritual impact that traumatic experiences have on us.

As God began to guide me toward deliverance and healing, I started to comprehend how trauma served as the gateway for fear to dominate my life. When I reflect on my past, the first time I remember feeling terrified was due to a traumatic experience. I understand that this book addresses sexual trauma, but it is important to note that this issue is not solely caused by sexual trauma.

Due to early exposure to various traumatic events during

my childhood, I learned to let fear dominate my thoughts. When I was younger, I developed compulsions as a result of anxiety stemming from fear. I often worried that someone close to me would die or be seriously injured, or that something else terrible would happen to me. So, a habitual fear or the spirit of fear eventually became the conduit for a lifelong struggle with anxiety and depression.

In my early 20s, I was diagnosed with complex PTSD (Post-Traumatic Stress Disorder) and BP II (Bipolar Disorder II). These two diagnoses came as a result of an on-the-job trauma, during which my mind had reached its limit of traumatic experiences and snapped. This was both a physical (medical) and spiritual crisis. I went through years of treatments, prescription medications, 'self-medication', and 3 psychiatric inpatient stays trying to find a solution, but nothing seemed to work; I suffered for a very long time.

Zara's story is a true account of an event that occurred to someone else. That situation opened the door to fear in her life, and she was never the same. Rarely leaving home and declining to go on family trips were signs that she had been living with fear for so long that anxiety and worry had become common experiences for her. She had lived that way for so long that she had forgotten the original incident, but the effects still remained because she had not sought help and allowed herself to heal.

Imagine all of the experiences in life that fear and anxiety have taken away from Zara. What if God's calling for Zara's life was for her to travel the globe, helping and making a positive impact on the lives of people? That one incident was allowed to destroy her entire destiny.

This brings me to the main point that I want to make about fear: Fear is a demonic assignment. The enemy doesn't have to do anything else to make you self-destruct. Once the seed has been planted early and it grows over time, most people, by default, will forever toggle back and forth between what God has called them to do, but fear keeps them from doing it. By the time they recognize what fear has robbed them of (if they ever recognize it), most are older in life. They have lived long enough not to care anymore, but they are not in good health to fulfill the call of God, had they come to the same conclusion and realization earlier in life.

John 16:33 says:

"... In the world you will have tribulation; but be of
good cheer, I have overcome the world."- NKJV

Now, can I share a harsh truth that we often avoid acknowledging within the Christian community? The truth is, we were never promised a life without trials and tribulations. In fact, we were told to expect them.

Take a look at another verse, 1 Peter 4:12-13:

"Beloved, do not think it strange concerning the fiery
trial which is to try you, as though some strange
thing happened to you; but rejoice to the extent
that you partake of Christ's sufferings, that when
His glory is revealed, you may also be glad with
exceeding joy." -NKJV

I used to ask myself, "Why me? Why has my life always been so hard?" During one of my pity parties, a friend asked me, "Who would you recommend?" At first, I didn't understand what she was asking, until she clarified. She said, "If you are undeserving of this hard life, who would you recommend to take your place? Who is deserving?"

That was my point. I felt that no one deserved to suffer. I wouldn't wish my experiences on anyone, and I certainly didn't want to have to go through them myself.

I couldn't fathom why God would allow so much pain, but that revealed my lack of understanding regarding the nature of God and the consequences of sin that came into the world after the fall of man. Even Tamar's situation was a result of the consequences of sin and living in a fallen world. The necessity for Jesus to die on the cross for us was to bear the consequences of sin for us.

Fear is present because of sin. So, when God says that He has not given us a spirit of fear, He is indicating that fear was not intended to be a part of His original design for us. When God made Adam and Eve, fear was not a part of their DNA. It wasn't until they were tricked by the enemy that fear was allowed to enter, as it is one of the primary tools the enemy uses to make people of God neglect or abandon their God-given assignments.

Before we are born, God has a plan for our lives. The enemy's job is to prevent it from happening. Many people have assignments in their lives that are given and ordained by God, but the presence of fear has hindered them from fulfilling those callings. Because of fear, many people have passed away without ever accomplishing or becoming all that they were created to be.

As I've grown, I've come to understand that what I was meant to do with my life for the glory of God would always be in direct opposition to what the enemy desired for me to accomplish. The enemy's plan against me, you, and every believer is to do whatever is necessary to dismantle and destroy our effectiveness in God. Why do most of us experience these traumas beginning in childhood? Evil does not play fair. There are no rules or limits for evil; that's why it's evil. Hell has an assignment, and that is to steal, kill, and destroy us and everything attached to us.

Fear launches an assault on our thoughts, resources, and future. It preys on our weaknesses and whispers lies of defeat in our ears. Recognize that fear is an enemy. It seeks to capture our minds and cripple us. But we serve a God greater than fear, and His power resides within us. We must acknowledge the presence of fear and not avoid addressing it. When we bring our fears into the light, we take away their power over us.

As believers, we must know that fear can infiltrate our lives following any traumatic or terrifying experience. By being aware of this, we can empower ourselves to make positive changes by seeking help when necessary. We must remember that healing is a process, and facing our fears is a courageous step towards freedom.

"For God has not given us a spirit of fear, but of power and of love and of a sound mind." 2 Timothy 1:7 NKJV

Healing Anger

Ms. Sandra was old enough to be my grandmother, but she was full of spunk and life. She had been in and out of the system and had stories that dated back to the 70s, chock full of drugs, partying, celebrities, and what she called the good times. She had been using cocaine since the late 60s, a little heroin, and started using crack in the early 80s, which became her drug of choice for almost three decades.

As sweet and kind as Ms. Sandra was, she had a vicious mean streak. You could be laughing with her one day; the next day, she could be so abrasive and cold. When I encounter people like this, I just assume that there's more to the story, and try not to treat them any differently.

Ms. Sandra and I grew quite close. We would talk, and she would tell me about the good old days. One day, I made the mistake (or perhaps not) of asking her if was as lively as a child as she is now. Ms. Sandra's demeanor changed. I watched as she clenched her fist as if she were contemplating hitting me, and I quickly apologized. I apologized to her for unintentionally offending her. Ms. Sandra walked away without saying anything else to me.

I didn't hear from her for the rest of the day. The next day, Ms. Sandra popped up. She was her usual animated and fun self. She treated me as if what had happened had never occurred. During our time together, Ms. Sandra became very quiet and asked if she could share something with me. So, of course, I said yes.

Ms. Sandra apologized for what happened the last time I saw her. Then she proceeded to tell me about her childhood. How it was riddled with abuse: an evil uncle taking advantage of her, being called a liar when she tried to tell someone, and getting beaten for even suggesting that her uncle was a monster. It went on for years, the torture and anguish of being violated by someone she should have trusted.

She started fighting back when she reached an age where she had enough strength to defend herself. She eventually dropped out of school at the age of 16 and ran away from home for good. She found herself hundreds of miles away from Georgia on the streets of Detroit, where she was introduced to the fast-paced life of drugs, prostitution, and partying.

Mrs. Sandra cried and told me that she was only a little girl. How could a little girl be about something like that? She said her family resented her for even bringing it up. Ms. Sandra said, "Those types of things were hush-hush when I was growing up; we didn't talk about stuff like that." She mentioned that she was asked by a cousin if she thought she was the only woman in the family that it happened to. She was told to get over it like everyone else because nothing would be done about it. This was the culture of that time, where the saying "what goes on in this house [good or bad] stays in this house" prevailed.

Over the years, Ms. Sandra admitted to stabbing people, carrying guns, and associating with individuals who had the ability to "make you disappear". She said she made up her mind after running away from home that no one would ever take advantage of her again. She would get them before they got her.

I believe the saddest part of her story, for me, was realizing that her family did believe her. Ms. Sandra was part of a generational issue where things were not talked about or dealt with. As a result, she was forced to hold onto the pain that she desperately wanted to release.

People thought Ms. Sandra was mean, but she was just misunderstood. She had gone through some experiences from which she never healed. She had pretty much given up hope that anything would change. I told Ms. Sandra that I believed her, and she burst into tears like a baby. She needed to hear that.

"Be angry, and do not sin": do not let the sun go down on your wrath, nor give place to the devil." Ephesians 4:26-27 NKJV

Anger alone is not a sin. It's what you do when you get angry that determines whether you have sinned or not. Ephesians 4:26-27 can be challenging for some individuals as it is easy to become angry, but difficult to avoid sinning when consumed by anger. A lot of the uncontrollable behaviors, such as anger, that we witness in individuals who have experienced sexual trauma are often attributed to a concept known as emotional dysregulation.

Emotional dysregulation simply means that you have difficulty controlling your feelings, emotions, and impulses. High levels of stress, like those experienced during traumatic experiences, affect how the brain functions. Stress produces chemicals such as cortisol in our bodies, which have been linked to physical health problems as well as mental health issues like depression and anxiety.

Most trauma victims will admit that their traumatic experiences made them feel helpless, defeated, or lacking control over their situation. In an attempt to avoid experiencing these emotions again, people often act hostile or aggressively to hide their other feelings, such as anxiety in situations they believe are beyond their control. I once heard someone say that yelling and screaming is the cry of the unheard. People who yell and fuss a lot often feel unheard at their core.

There was a time when I had to attend anger management classes due to some legal trouble I got into because my anger was out of control. After receiving the diagnosis of Bipolar II Disorder and learning that the agitation I experienced, which led me to act the way I did, was referred to as a "mixed" state. I was feeling depressed and overwhelmed by a mix of emotions, which led me to become easily irritated and react impulsively. Well, I did think about it. However, in that moment, I felt a strong desire to express my point of view and be heard. Unfortunately, my frustration caused me to act irrationally.

Anger is often referred to as a secondary emotion because it stems from another emotion, specifically a primary emotion that may make us feel vulnerable and weak. Anger expressions stem from an attempt to appear strong and in control of a situation that we may otherwise feel too inadequate to handle.

Because of my PTSD diagnosis, I was given the opportunity to participate in anger management sessions alongside other professionals who also had PTSD. Most of them were military or law enforcement personnel. It wasn't until I joined this group that I was able to connect my rage and anger outbursts to my mental health issues, which were initially triggered by repeated traumatic experiences. It was a response to trauma.

Sidebar:

The "angry black woman" label that some black women exhibit is an example of a trauma response, and often, that trauma runs deeper than she would ever admit. Like Ms. Sandra's voice, many voices have been silenced at a young age, and people have become accustomed to concealing trauma and pain in their lives. So it manifests in various ways, such as anger. Even if a person doesn't utter a word, their body aches to tell the story and be heard. Trauma is known to attach itself to individuals and reside within the body. As temples of God, our bodies were not created to house trauma. So, anger manifested can also be seen as the body trying to release what shouldn't be there. If left unaddressed, anger can reach a point where it can transcend into the spiritual realm of demonic oppression and, in extreme cases, even demonic possession.

In my years working with juveniles, I encountered many angry children. There was a boy who went on an arson binge, but then there was another one that I will never forget. This particular incident serves as an example of just how powerful an angry, demonically possessed person can be.

This guy was in his early teens. He had to serve time because of his anger issues. He would become so angry that he would zone out, and you never really knew what to expect. His latest episode resulted in significant destruction. When he was calm, he was actually a really well-behaved child, but when he became angry, there was a different side to him. He would always say, "I don't know. Things just happen when I get mad. I don't always remember."

For some reason, he harbored an intense hatred for his parents. He thought he would be released into the custody of his grandparents, but when he found out he would have to go home to his parents, he was furious. He was informed that there would be a meeting with his family and a case manager before his release. He did not want to meet with them, and the more information he was given, the more frustrated he became.

As the meeting time arrived, the boy said in a very monotone voice, "This shouldn't take long," and he entered the office with the case manager and his parents. Well, they were in the room with his parents for maybe 10 minutes before the case manager and parents ran out of the room screaming. The boy walked out behind them, appearing very calm, but with the most devious smile on his face.

When the commotion died down, we learned that the boy had expressed his anger and requested to leave the session. When they refused, the boy threatened to end the session if they didn't comply. The boy then proceeded to count backward from 10. He told them the lights would go out when he reached 1. They ignored him, believing he was having a "moment." To their surprise, when the boy reached 1, the lights went out and would not come back on; the session was over.

His parents were afraid of him. I'm not quite sure what happened to that boy, but I know he didn't go home.

How often do we hear people who commit heinous crimes claim that something took over them, that all they saw was red, or that they blacked out? These are all signs of demonic influence, all possible if anger is not properly addressed and allowed to fester. For trauma survivors, that means addressing the underlying issues that trigger episodes of anger. We handle them in order to avoid suffering from their consequences. While trauma, hurt, and pain may be at the root of anger for many, the negative manifestations of anger have destroyed relationships and caused people to lose their jobs, livelihoods, and freedom.

It is essential to recognize that seeking help is not a sign of weakness, but rather a courageous step towards reclaiming our lives and finding freedom from the burdens of anger influenced by trauma. It might take some time, but it's worth addressing the anger issues. If you require a deeper exploration of anger and additional help, at the end of this section, I recommend the book "Deal With It: The Spirit of Anger" by Nori Moore. Nori Moore is a Certified Anger Management Specialist (CAMS-I) who also addresses the spiritual issues related to anger in more detail.

Remember, throughout this process, be gentle with yourself. Healing takes time, and setbacks may occur. However, always keep in mind that God's love and grace are ever-present, offering us hope, restoration, and transformation.

"So then, my beloved brethren, let every man be swift to hear, slow to speak, slow to wrath; for the wrath of man does not produce the righteousness of God." - James 1:19-20 NKJV

RECOMMENDED READING:
"Deal With It: The Spirit of Anger" By Nori Moore
Published by Bowker, 2021[1]

---

1. 1. Nori Moore, *Deal With It: The Spirit of Anger* (Tallahassee, FL: Bowker, 2021).

Reclaiming Our Voices

COURAGE TO SPEAK

"You may encounter many defeats, but you must not be defeated."
- Maya Angelou[1]

When we experience trauma, there is often a profound sense of powerlessness and silence that accompanies it. Our voices are silenced, our stories hidden away, and our pain kept in the shadows.

There's a difference between having the ability to speak and having a voice. The ability to speak refers to the physical capability of producing sounds and words through vocalization. However, having a voice means having the agency, courage, and opportunity to share your ideas, opinions, and experiences openly and authentically. It involves having a sense of empowerment, feeling heard, and making a difference in the world.

When Maya Angelou was seven years old, she was raped by her mother's boyfriend. When asked who did it, she gave his name. He spent a single day in jail but was ultimately killed less than a week after being released. I saw a clip of an old interview from the Oprah Winfrey Show where Maya Angelou[2] said:

> "I thought my voice killed that man, and that my voice was so evil that if I put it out, it could kill anybody."

Maya Angelou would suffer from mutism for the next five years.

The effects of sexual trauma are far-reaching, but one of the most significant impacts I've witnessed in others and myself is how trauma snuffs out your voice. It makes you feel that you have nothing significant to say, and if you have something to say, it doesn't matter because who would listen to you? Who would care to hear what you have to say? These are the lies that trauma tells. For women of faith, your voice is often tied to your God-given ministry. So to snuff out your voice young is to snuff out your effectiveness within the kingdom of God.

I was writing at a very young age because those feelings consumed me. As someone with a prophetic voice as it relates to wisdom, revelation, and exhortation, I rejected the prophetic ministry in my life. I mean, what type of prophet doesn't speak? I've always been very observant, and the longer I live and walk with God, the more I encounter prophetic voices that the enemy attempts to silence and cripple at a young age so that they never fully understand who they are. And if, by chance, they did come to recognize who they are in Christ, they would never be able to carry it out fully because their voices were stolen.

As horrible as sexual assault is, as believers, we must recognize the assignment from hell that it attempts to carry out over our lives.

When we experience trauma, our voices are often silenced, and our pain remains hidden. But there is a profound difference between having the ability to speak and genuinely having a voice. As Maya Angelou eloquently stated, we may encounter defeats, but we must not be defeated. The journey of healing from trauma involves reclaiming our voice and recognizing the lies that trauma tells us.

For those who have experienced the suffocating grip of trauma, know that your voice matters. Your pain, your story, and your healing journey have the potential to ignite hope, bring healing to others, and glorify God. Embrace the truth of who you are in Christ, and know that your voice, when unleashed, can break chains, dismantle darkness, and bring transformation. May you find the strength to rise above the lies of trauma, reclaim your voice, and step into the fullness of your calling. You are a warrior, an overcomer, and a beacon of hope. Your voice matters, and the world needs to hear it.

"The Spirit of the Lord God is upon Me Because the Lord has anointed Me. To preach good tidings to the poor; He has sent Me to heal the brokenhearted, To proclaim liberty to the captives, And the opening of the prison to those who are bound;"
-Isaiah 61:1 NKJV

1. 1. "A Quote by Maya Angelou," Goodreads, accessed August 2, 2023, https://www.goodreads.com/quotes/93512-you-may-encounter-many-defeats-but-you-must-not-be.
2. 1. "Maya Angelou on Becoming Mute in the Aftermath of Childhood Trauma | the Oprah Winfrey Show | Own," YouTube, August 24, 2019, https://www.youtube.com/watch?v=IV2lZw--_l4&t=24s.

Breaking Free from Guilt and Shame

When I was seven years old, my family lived on a military base in Oakland, CA. Our home was located on the second floor of a tri-level apartment-style military housing building. A family moved into the first floor - very strange people with a house full of girls. I didn't like them because they were all older than me and quite mean, especially the middle girl.

She appeared to be around 13 or maybe 14 years old, and she made it her mission to antagonize me every day. Whenever she saw me outside alone, she would come out to watch me play and stare at me in an intimidating way, which made me feel uncomfortable. After months of observing me, she finally started to engage in conversation. Every day, she would ask me the same question: "Do you like milk?" or "Would you care for some milk?" I would consistently ignore her and continue riding my bike. She asked me the questions so often that I eventually stopped going outside when I knew she was around. I looked out our window to see if she was near the exit door. If I don't see her, I will run out to the playground or the basketball court.

That seemed to do the trick until I noticed her peeking

out of her window, observing me as I walked back home. She would carefully observe my every move until she started meeting me outside once more. She would wait until I entered the building to ask me silly questions about milk. Finally, one day, I grew weary of her constant inquiries about milk and firmly expressed my disdain for it, stating that I hated milk. I quickly learned that she was not talking about milk at all. She told me she wasn't referring to cow's milk, but rather her own breast milk. She offered me some and even squeezed her breast in my direction.

At 7 years old, I did not understand what she meant by extracting milk from her breasts. She continued to harass me until one day when she cornered me in the hallway. She proposed that she would leave me alone if I could defeat her younger sister in a bike race. I agreed to a race because I wanted her to leave me alone. I did not know that she had instructed her sister to win at all costs, even if it meant causing me harm.

As we raced, I pedaled as fast as possible until I felt a thumping against my rear tire. I skidded and wobbled, but I didn't fall. Their sister was ramming her bike against mine as if she were auditioning for The Fast and the Furious. She collided with my bike so forcefully that the pedal of her bicycle became stuck and tangled in my wheel. I was afraid of falling. I wasn't necessarily scared of getting hurt, but I didn't want those girls to do anything to me. So, I pedaled hard and started to lift my front wheel, attempting to perform a catwalk maneuver to untangle her pedal. Our bikes were forcefully separated, and the girl was thrown off her bike. She skidded and rolled across the gravel and concrete. It was an ugly and bloody scene.

I looked back and saw her lying on the road. I wanted to stop and help, but I kept riding towards the finish line because

I needed to win. That was the deal: if I won, her sister would leave me alone.

At the age of seven, I was unaware that it was possible to be groomed by another child. As an adult counselor, I recognize that she may have been groomed and potentially harmed by someone else. The aggressor was becoming the victim. I have a history of experiencing sexual assault from both males and females. These perplexing incidents led to uncertainty about my sexuality at a very young age.

It was embarrassing for me to be violated by someone of the opposite sex. But there was a profound sense of shame that came with being violated by someone of the same sex. It felt as if no amount of showers could wash it away, as if I hadn't fought back hard enough or done everything I could.

We often feel guilt and shame because we convince ourselves that we have more control and influence in a situation than we actually do. They say that hindsight is 20/20, but honestly, we often deceive ourselves about the true nature of innocence. Innocence is characterized by naivety, trustworthiness, love, and kindness. Our perspective on the world is altered when we possess innocence; it becomes pure. The people who violate others lose their pure worldview before inflicting destruction upon others. Their vision has been impaired and misaligned. So, guilt and shame on the part of the victims are self-defeating.

I've heard many times, mainly in church circles, that guilt and shame are rooted in pride. While that may be true in some circumstances, there is a form of guilt and shame that stems from humiliation, feeling weak, and powerless.

Feelings of guilt can arise from a sense of remorse or responsibility for past actions (or inaction) or behaviors that have caused harm to oneself or others. In contrast, shame can arise from a profound feeling of unworthiness or inadequacy, where individuals perceive their very essence as flawed or fundamentally deficient.

But the truth is, the guilt and shame we often carry as survivors are not ours to bear. We blame ourselves for not doing enough to defend or advocate for ourselves, causing us to internalize the impact of the actions imposed upon us. Guilt and shame are tactics the enemy uses to keep us trapped and divert blame away from the true culprits. We have to recognize that the fault lies with the perpetrators, more specifically, the motivation behind their actions.

> "Then Tamar put ashes on her head, and tore her robe
> of many colors that was on her, and laid her hand
> on her head and went away crying bitterly." 2
> Samuel 13:19 NKJV

My McArthur Study Bible explains verse 19:

> "The ashes were a sign of mourning. The torn garment
> symbolizes the ruin of her life. The hand on the head
> was emblematic of exile and banishment. The crying
> showed that she viewed herself as good as dead."

What Tamar experienced, and her reaction, stemmed a lot from the culture of that day. What Ammon did to her caused her to lose her virginity, which was highly valued. Failing to be a virgin greatly reduced her chances of getting married. During this time, women were mainly expected to focus on domestic duties. Being unmarried and without a husband often meant living in poverty, not having children, and occupying the lowest position in society.

While that may not be the case now, the essence of that passage still lives on and manifests itself through guilt and shame in the lives of survivors today.

By recognizing that these emotions related to traumatic experiences may arise from societal expectations, we can start questioning their legitimacy. Turning to Scripture, we can find the truth of our worth and identity in God's eyes by embracing His grace and forgiveness. By challenging negative beliefs and replacing them with the truth of God's love, we can develop a mindset grounded in freedom and acceptance.

There is therefore now no condemnation to those who are in Christ Jesus, who do not walk according to the flesh, but according to the Spirit. -Romans 8:1 NKJV

Breaking the Stigma

"It is easier to say "My tooth is aching" than to say "My heart is broken." —— C.S. Lewis

---

Mental illness is often demonized. It's unfortunate that there is a stigma surrounding mental health conditions, which causes many individuals to refrain from seeking the necessary help they truly need. I've heard people ignorantly claim that ALL mental health issues are a sign of possession or a lack of faith. To clarify, sickness is not the will of God in any form. However, in this fallen world, sickness persists for the same reason as other undesirable things - sin.

Don't get me wrong, there are cases of demonic possession, and it can sometimes mimic or manifest as various illnesses. However, the problem arises when people *wrongly* attribute mental health issues to possession. This is one of the misconceptions that contribute to the stigma surrounding mental health among people of faith. We tend to overemphasize the demonic aspect in these situations, whereas we wouldn't do the same for physical illnesses such as high blood pressure, heart disease, cancer, or diabetes. It's essential to remember that the brain is an organ, just like the heart, lungs, or kidneys, and it can experience issues that may require treatment.

As a substance abuse counselor, I have frequently encountered clients with co-occurring disorders, which means they struggle with both substance use and mental health issues. Depression, anxiety, bipolar disorder, PTSD, schizophrenia, and excessive stress are among the most common disorders I encounter. Substance use assessments will often show a need for referrals to a mental health professional if one is necessary.

It's incredible to witness how proper treatment can transform people's lives. I have witnessed individuals who previously did not believe in God undergo treatment and find faith, embrace Christianity, and even become actively involved in ministry. So, I'm open to the idea that healing can manifest in various ways, and it is important to discuss this within faith communities. This dialogue should not only be limited to individuals with sexual trauma but should also be open to anyone struggling with mental illness who may be hesitant to speak up due to fear of judgment or stigma.

It is concerning that over the past decade, there has been an increase in pastors suffering from depression, and some have even resorted to committing suicide. Just imagine attempting to preach and teach the word of God, shepherd a congregation, and provide support to others while simultaneously struggling with severe depression, trauma, addiction, or other challenges, all without receiving the proper help. I understand that some of these ideas originate from faith-based communities, while others stem from cultural beliefs or generational understanding. These factors often discourage people from seeking help.

The older generations are less likely to receive the

assistance they require. Women are more likely than men to receive the help they need. Certain ethnic groups, such as Native Americans, are less likely to receive treatment. The bottom line is that many groups avoid seeking help, and as a result, they experience unnecessary suffering. Sometimes, the situation is bigger than us to shoulder on our own because it wasn't meant for us to carry alone.

This leads me to my point that ***trauma has to be treated.***

Trauma must be treated by addressing both the physical and spiritual aspects. When someone experiences sexual trauma, it affects both their physical and spiritual well-being.

I've seen people solely focus on the physical (natural man) aspect of healing, seeking therapy, joining support groups, and sometimes even going to inpatient facilities. However, they often seem to cycle through the system without ever fully healing. They learn how to go through the motions, becoming programmed to perform certain tasks, but they never experience the internal transformation that accompanies deliverance and healing.

On the other hand, some people solely seek spiritual help without addressing their physical needs. After experiencing deliverance, there are things that you have to relearn in order to maintain your healing and deliverance. When individuals solely focus on their spiritual needs while neglecting their physical needs, they often find themselves questioning the depth of their faith, the effectiveness of their prayers, and the significance of fasting.

They can begin to fall into the cycle of constantly seeking a "deeper" and "more" spiritual experience, which can eventually turn their spiritual life into an addictive cycle. A dose of prayer, a dose of worship, a dose of church service, a dose of giving, rinse, and repeat. The same compulsive behaviors that can occur with substance abuse or other vices can also manifest in faith-based activities. Going through the motions may give the average onlooker the illusion that a person has it all together because they know how to practice religion. However, in reality, the person is in need of help.

This also places unrealistic expectations on the church because if their efforts do not succeed, it can lead to disillusionment with both the church and their faith. We are living in a time when many people have become disillusioned with the church and have started to deconstruct their faith because of misattributions and a lack of understanding of the church's purpose.

Before closing this section on the emotional effects of trauma, I want to emphasize the importance of therapy for people who have undergone traumatic experiences. I remember my early twenties when I first began trauma therapy. I would consistently revert to hazy memories of my youth. After some probing, my therapist realized the extent to which trauma had hindered my emotional development.

She was a trauma expert, and she explained that we stop growing emotionally at the age of our first unhealed trauma. So, if someone experiences abuse at the age of 12 and never seeks help or healing, their emotional intelligence (EQ) might remain stagnant at that 12-year-old age, longing for support, affection, and healing. In essence, they are adults with the emotional baggage of their childhood, still carrying the wounds of their past.

In some cases, people resort to drugs or alcohol as a means of self-medication and to numb emotional pain. This pattern of substance abuse can be inherited within families. If parents have a history of substance abuse or use substances to cope with their problems, their children are more likely to develop similar issues. Still, God has the power to heal and deliver.

In closing, remember that our faith journey is not one of isolation but of connection - with God, others, and ourselves.

Trials and afflictions, including mental health struggles and substance use disorders, do not necessarily indicate spiritual failure. Instead, they are a natural part of our human experience. Our healing journeys may be challenging, but they provide opportunities for personal growth, understanding, and a deeper connection with God. Every part of the Body of Christ must be cared for and nurtured uniquely, as we all have unique needs.

"For I consider that the sufferings of this present time are not worthy *to be compared* with the glory which shall be revealed in us. For the earnest expectation of the creation eagerly waits for the revealing of the sons of God. For the creation was subjected to futility, not willingly, but because of Him who subjected *it* in hope; because the creation itself also will be delivered from the bondage of corruption into the glorious liberty of the children of God."

-Romans 8:18-21 NKJV

Part Two

～～

RELATIONAL EFFECTS

What are Relational Effects?

"After being hurt, you learn to build walls for anyone who dares to get too close. Trust becomes a distant dream.[1]" - Unknown

Building and sustaining relationships has always been a challenge for me. When I notice people getting too close, I tend to withdraw. I don't want people to get too close to me because those who I have allowed to get close have been the ones responsible for hurting me. So, to protect myself, I learned to only reveal enough of myself to put people at ease, but never enough to expose my vulnerability. That's how I protect myself from hurt, betrayal, loss of trust, and the feeling of foolishness for falling for someone's facade. That's my truth, as people say. Now that I've explained it, I would ask any other survivor if they can relate to any of these emotions.

Truth is, the one thing that is most damaged when someone takes advantage of you is your ability to trust. Yet, the foundation of building a strong, healthy relationship with a person in any capacity is trust, which is the one thing that most survivors struggle with. The pain caused by someone we should have been able to trust can make us question the motives and intentions of everyone who enters our life thereafter. They had nothing to do with the situation, but we constructed barriers of protection around our hearts and emotions to avoid experiencing the feelings of letdown, defeat, disappointment, frustration, and anger that come with someone betraying our trust.

So, when I mention the relational effects of sexual trauma, this is what I am referring to: those emotions that we experience as a result of trauma and that we allow to influence our relationships with others. Situations where the dynamics between two people influence how each person perceives themselves and experiences life. Whether it's a friendship, romantic partnership, family bond, or any other relationship, these connections deeply affect our emotional and psychological well-being.

The relationships we form act as mirrors, reflecting our deepest selves and influencing how we perceive ourselves, the world, and our place within it. They can be a source of joy and, at times, deep pain. Understanding the impact of sexual trauma enables us to approach the intricacy of relational dynamics with empathy and respect. The journey through trust issues, intimacy struggles, commitment apprehensions, power imbalances, transference issues, communication boundaries, and vulnerability is undoubtedly challenging, and it manifests differently in the lives of individuals.

In this section, my goal is not to cover every single relationship situation but rather to provide enough information about the effects so that individuals can start examining their own lives. By doing so, they may be able to identify red flags or patterns within their relationships that could be rooted in past traumatic experiences. Some of the stories I share may be triggering for some individuals. If that's the case, there may be sections that you need to skip over if they are too heavy for you. The overall goal is not to further traumatize people through shock value but to depict true-life scenarios that many people live with, which may have been overlooked or ignored.

The pain inflicted by those we should have trusted casts a long shadow, making it difficult to open up. Yet, recognizing these struggles is the first step toward deliverance and healing. As we embark on this journey, we will navigate the complexities of trust, intimacy, communication, and vulnerability with empathy and respect. Despite the hurdles, understanding the impact of trauma on our relationships can guide us to a state of resilience, fortitude, and self-discovery.

---

1. Unknown, "After being hurt, you learn to build walls for anyone who dares to get too close. Trust becomes a distant dream."

Barriers to Vulnerability

Monica's motto was, "Don't trust no n-[words]". She was quick to let you know that she didn't trust anyone because everyone was only out for themselves, so she felt the need to protect herself. Now, people may pass a lot of judgment on Monica because she was definitely rough around the edges and had a very strong personality. She could be combative at times, but no one knew the darkness that lurked beneath her tough and offensive exterior, revealing the hardships she faced in her life.

When Monica was a little girl, her mom lost custody of her due to her addiction. As a result, Monica's dad was granted full custody. He eventually remarried a woman who had a son. Her stepmom had a 12-year-old son, but she and Monica's dad would also have a second son together. Her stepmom never tried to replace her mother, but showed her as much love and compassion as she could. Monica loved her stepmother very much. Life was great until her baby brother turned four and started school. His stepmother stopped being a stay-at-home wife and mother and returned to part-time work, picking up a few evening shifts at the hotel.

Monica's dad was a supervisor at the local shipyard, and he also played the drums as a music minister in several local churches. He would often get called to play at revivals, conferences, and other services during the week, which provided extra income for the family.

With the overlapping schedules, the responsibility of babysitting fell on her older stepbrother, who was now 16 and mature. Monica was old enough at the time to make a sandwich and take care of her own hygiene needs. She was quite self-sufficient, so her stepbrother didn't have much to do. He spent a lot of time playing video games and making sure their younger brother stayed out of trouble, a task that Monica often assisted with as well.

Everything was good, and then it wasn't. He began coming into her bedroom unannounced, and from there it led to molestation. It didn't happen every day, but multiple times a week. One day, her stepmother came home a little early and caught him leaving her room.

She confronted Monica about him being there, and Monica told the truth about what he had been doing to her. The stepmother called her a whore and accused her of lying. She told her she was being fast, and insinuated that their non-biological sibling relationship was not a justification for engaging in sexual activity. Her stepmother told her father what had happened, and they both agreed that it was best for Monica to go live with her mother.

Her mother still wasn't stable and eventually lost custody of Monica again. However, this time Monica was sent to a group home, where she would encounter many more individuals similar to her stepbrother until she aged out of the system.

Monica's journey has been defined by the sting of betrayal, a burden that continued to haunt her well into her thirties, causing her to struggle with the concept of trust and the ability to embrace love. There was a man who genuinely cared for her and desired to walk the path of marriage with her. However, she approached him with a guarded heart, as if he were an adversary. Her hesitation stemmed not from his actions, because he had done nothing to warrant doubt, but rather from the scars left by others. Those scars had etched a pattern of shielding herself from harm, making it difficult for her to reveal her vulnerabilities and affections.

Vulnerability, the essence of openness and authenticity, serves as the foundation upon which connections are built. Yet, for those who have survived the horrors of sexual trauma, vulnerability morphs into a treacherous minefield, with each step threatening to reopen wounds that time should have healed. Sexual trauma has the power to transform vulnerability into an overwhelming obstacle.

The ability to embrace vulnerability necessitates a certain level of trust and a willingness to disclose aspects of oneself without fear of negative consequences or manipulation. This capacity for vulnerability proves essential in the formation of deep relationships, as it acts as a bridge between people. However, for those affected by the experience of sexual trauma, the notion of exposing one's innermost self and embracing others can be daunting. The wounds run deep.

The impact of sexual trauma extends to the realm of emotions, lingering long after the traumatic event has occurred. Survivors often struggle with a sense of insecurity and self-doubt. At the outset, mechanisms of self-preservation, such as suppressing emotions or building walls, provide comfort. Yet, over time, these very defenses make it difficult to embrace future relationships.

A significant barrier to vulnerability for survivors is the

fear of being rejected or betrayed again. The fracture of trust caused by sexual trauma casts shadows over survivors' perceptions of others' intentions. Allowing vulnerability entails lowering defenses, which can be overwhelming for survivors, as they fear experiencing past pain again. As a safeguard, some might withdraw, maintaining a vigilant guard, perceiving the sharing of intimate emotions as a gamble, a risk too great to take.

Shame and self-blame often plague survivors, further complicating their feelings of vulnerability. Society's misguided finger-pointing reinforces these feelings, fostering a sense of unworthiness that hinders love and understanding. The healing journey necessitates a certain level of vulnerability, an ability to forgive others, and perhaps even more challenging, ourselves. Trust forms the cornerstone of vulnerability, and its absence often indicates lingering resentment. If the shadows from the past wield power over the present, their grip remains strong enough to influence the present.

In the situation I mentioned, the interaction between trust and betrayal manifests as a struggle with vulnerability. Past breaches of trust cast a long shadow over future relationships, even though the present individuals may bear no responsibility for the pain inflicted. Unresolved trauma distorts vulnerability across the spectrum, causing some individuals to approach others with caution, while others refuse to trust anyone, including their spouse. This lack of trust can transform into an expectation of betrayal, leading to unfair accusations against partners or embracing falsehoods.

Isaiah 43:18-19 (NIV) imparts a powerful message:

"Forget the former things; do not dwell on the past."
See, I am doing a new thing! Now it springs up; do you not perceive it? I am making a way in the wilderness and streams in the wasteland."

This scripture offers a guiding light, urging us to let go of the past and embrace the new chapters that God is writing. It underscores God's remarkable ability to usher in transformation and rebirth, even in the harshest of circumstances. In the context of rebuilding trust through God's grace, it emphasizes the need to unshackle ourselves from the clutches of past traumas and hurts. The verse urges us to reject the temptation of pain and negativity, as God is creating a new story filled with hope and rejuvenation.

These words imply that God labors ceaselessly, carving pathways in the desolate wilderness and breathing life into barren lands. Even where life appears unyielding and desolation rules, God orchestrates rejuvenation, healing, and revival. The confines of past experiences and the fragments of shattered trust do not confine God's ability to forge a new path, infusing the voids with His benevolence, grace, and redemption.

Centering our focus on God's transformative prowess and His knack for sculpting beauty from the forge of adversity instills hope and reassurance. It is a call to trust that, as we relinquish control to God's hand, He will mend and restore, tearing down the barriers that hinder our ability to be vulnerable.

"There is no fear in love; but perfect love casts out fear, because fear involves torment. But he who fears has not been made perfect in love." 1 John 4:18

Trading Trauma for Tolerance

I once met a young girl who never spoke up in her relationship. She would tell stories about her child's father and how he treated her. He was extremely controlling, and she was not allowed to go anywhere without his permission. Whenever she left the house, he would meticulously calculate the time it would take for her to reach her destination, and then call her to confirm that she had arrived within the exact timeframe he had calculated.

She couldn't see her family when she wanted to and had to make sure that his needs were met before she could tend to her own. He told her that he was the head of the household and that she was supposed to submit to his authority. She spoke about these things as if they were normal as if she were proud to have such a caring man.

When I told her that her relationship didn't seem as healthy as she portrayed it, she responded, "It could be worse." Curious, I asked her how much worse it could be. She revealed that her previous boyfriend used to physically abuse her, whereas her current boyfriend (who is not her husband) does not. So, I asked her whether her current situation was actually healthy or if it was simply an improvement compared to her previous relationship. She dropped her head and told me, "I've never been asked that before. I never thought of that."

This is a common theme I've witnessed over the years: people often remain in unfavorable circumstances because, although the situation is not ideal, it is still better than what they have previously endured. So, they perceive an improvement from one situation to the next as progress, without realizing that they are merely replacing one form of abuse with another.

Trauma prevents people from being able to exercise and execute sound judgment in their situations. Abuse has the tendency to cause people to lower their standards for what they truly deserve in life. As a result, they find themselves settling for something that is below what they should tolerate and accept. Their trauma causes them to alter their decision-making process to one of tolerance, often accepting behavior that falls well below basic human standards. We teach people how to treat us based on what we tolerate.

Trading trauma for tolerance is a dangerous game because eventually, a person will grow tired of their needs being unmet. They may become resentful without understanding why, leading to feelings of bitterness, frustration, and anger. This toxic combination is often seen in episodes of "Snapped." Women who reach the breaking point, where they can no longer bear the situation, may explode like a powder keg and do something they end up regretting for the rest of their lives. Some of them end up spending the rest of their lives in prison because they reached their limit, failed to recognize the warning signs, and snapped.

During an inpatient psychiatric hospital stay over a decade ago, I had the pleasure of meeting a talented artist and singer. We connected because of our shared love for drawing, and she happened to attend one of the top art schools in the country. I would look at the pictures that she drew; she loved drawing eyes. She would ask me why I stared at her pictures so intensely. I explained to her that I could see the depth of her emotions through the eyes of the pictures she drew. I would later learn that she had attempted suicide. In fact, she confided in me that the doctors said it was a miracle she survived. They found her unconscious in a pool of vomit.

I learned that she had a history of sexual abuse and struggled with a constant feeling of inadequacy. In order to avoid feeling like a failure, she would settle for less than what she truly desired. This gave her a false sense of accomplishment, even though she was not truly fulfilled. She had learned to tolerate mediocrity because trauma had convinced her that, despite being more than capable of accomplishing her dreams, she did not have the ability to do more.

She possessed all the talents but lacked determination. Trauma had stripped her of her standards. She was miserable because, despite settling and being able to accomplish the small goals she set for herself, there was still an artist and singer within her who longed to travel the world and experience life wherever her talents would take her. But she had made the grave mistake of imprisoning herself in mediocrity.

She broke up with her boyfriend before attempting to take her own life. She said he believed in her too much, and she hated that he thought she was more than she actually was. She intentionally destroyed a relationship where someone was trying to help her out of her pit. She said that he began inviting her to the church when they first started dating. However, as she observed how influential he was with his music (he attended the same art school), she started feeling inadequate to be with him. She saw his greatness, but not her own.

She and I stayed in contact for many years afterward. She received counseling and started singing for several prominent gospel artists. Eventually, she and he reconciled and got back together. We lost contact. I'm not sure where she is now, but in that moment, it was amazing to see her start living instead of merely tolerating existence.

In Proverbs 3:5-6, we are encouraged to trust in the Lord with all our hearts and not rely on our own understanding. Even when we doubt ourselves, He knows our true worth. In our darkest moments, we may inadvertently push away those who genuinely care about us, just as the artist did when she left her boyfriend who believed in her. It's a tragic mistake born out of self-doubt. With faith and healing, we can break free from the prison of mediocrity and live the life we were meant to lead.

Remember, we are worth more than settling for less, and God's plan for us is one of purpose, fulfillment, and greatness.

———

" I will praise You, for I am fearfully *and* wonderfully made; Marvelous are Your works, And *that* my soul knows very well." - Psalm 139:14 NKJV

Roadblocks and Intimacy

Sarah was a traveling minister, a dynamic teacher, and a powerful prayer warrior. We could talk about the goodness of the Lord all day, every day, but her schedule was always swamped. Conferences in one city, revival services in another - her calendar was packed.

One day, I made a comment about how I couldn't imagine juggling such a demanding schedule while also having family responsibilities. Sarah responded by saying that her husband should understand her calling to ministry, and if he didn't, then it was a matter between him and God.

Despite our numerous conversations, something about the way Sarah spoke those words felt peculiar. There seemed to be a hint of resentment behind her remarks about her husband. I didn't mention it at the time.

Over the course of approximately a month, I began to notice an increasing number of red flags. Sarah's bitterness and resentment became increasingly evident and more difficult for her to hide. Eventually, she reached a breaking point and confessed that she was considering leaving her husband because he wanted to spend more quality time together.

I didn't see anything wrong with her husband's request, but Sarah struggled with it. She finally revealed that she hated it when her husband touched her. His affection felt suffocating, and she found it "disgusting."

As it turned out, Sarah had only gotten married because she felt it was expected of her as a devout woman. Her marriage had turned into a hellish experience because she was keeping a secret from her husband.

During her early childhood, she was molested by an older male relative. The pain of that violation and the repeated abuses haunted her for years until the abuse eventually stopped when she reached puberty. She suspected that the relative might have targeted another prepubescent child.

Later, during her time in the military, she felt the calling to ministry, but it didn't fully materialize until years later. In the meantime, she met a young man whom she loved and cared for. They got married and started a family together.

She couldn't pinpoint when or why it happened, but one day, during a moment of intimacy with her husband, she had a flashback to those traumatic moments from her childhood. From that day on, his touch became a trigger for her, forcing her to relive the worst experiences of her life.

As the years went by, she managed to convince herself that her ministry of traveling was God's work. However, deep down, she was unknowingly succumbing to the influence of her unresolved trauma.

AVOIDING INTIMACY

The avoidance of intimacy among people who have experienced sexual trauma can manifest in various ways. Firstly, they may encounter challenges in establishing and sustaining emotional intimacy with others. They may feel apprehensive about being vulnerable because it could trigger past traumatic experiences and lead to feelings of helplessness or powerlessness. Consequently, individuals may develop emotional barriers as a means of safeguarding themselves from potential harm, thereby concealing their true thoughts and emotions from others.

Secondly, individuals who have experienced sexual trauma may encounter difficulties in engaging in physical intimacy. They may encounter feelings of discomfort, anxiety, or fear when participating in physical contact, even in non-sexual contexts. This aversion to physical touch can be observed in individuals who actively avoid engaging in hugs, handshakes, or any form of close physical contact. Furthermore, individuals may develop a heightened sense of vigilance regarding personal boundaries, imposing strict restrictions on physical interactions to prevent the reactivation of traumatic memories.

Thirdly, the avoidance of intimacy can also manifest as difficulties related to trust. Individuals who have experienced sexual trauma may face difficulties in building trust with others, especially in the context of intimate relationships. They may possess ingrained suspicion, which is characterized by a fear of potential harm or betrayal from others. This can result in them hesitating to disclose personal information, express vulnerability, or rely on others for assistance. The fear of being vulnerable and the potential for re-traumatization can hinder their ability to form deep and meaningful connections with others.

Additionally, the act of avoiding intimacy may encompass behaviors such as withdrawing from social interactions or isolating from others. Those who have experienced sexual trauma may experience feelings of shame or self-blame, which can contribute to a belief that they are undeserving of love or connection. Consequently, they may choose to create emotional and physical distance from their peers due to their fear of being judged or rejected. This self-imposed isolation serves as a defensive mechanism, protecting them from potential emotional harm.

In general, those who have experienced sexual trauma often choose to avoid intimacy as a means of self-preservation and protecting themselves against potential further pain. It is of utmost importance to adopt a compassionate and empathetic approach when dealing with them, demonstrating understanding and patience. This approach will provide them with the necessary environment to heal and gradually regain their ability to trust and establish intimate connections. Professional support and therapy can significantly contribute to helping to effectively manage these challenges and make progress toward establishing healthier and more fulfilling relationships.

PROMISCUITY

After experiencing sexual trauma, it's common to struggle with a range of emotions and behaviors related to intimacy. These challenges can manifest through promiscuity, where a person engages in multiple sexual encounters or relationships without forming deep emotional connections.

For some survivors of sexual trauma, engaging in promiscuous behavior can serve as a coping mechanism or a means to regain control over their bodies and experiences. It might provide a temporary sense of power and control. However, it can also be an unconscious attempt to numb emotional pain or to seek validation and acceptance from others. Therefore, it is important to approach the topic of promiscuity with understanding and compassion, recognizing that it is a complex response to trauma that requires support and healing.

One characteristic of promiscuity is engaging in casual sexual encounters. Promiscuous individuals often prioritize physical pleasure or sexual gratification over emotional connection or intimacy. As a result, they may engage in sexual activities without seeking or desiring a committed relationship. These encounters may be brief or sporadic, focusing on immediate sexual satisfaction rather than on forming deeper emotional connections.

Another aspect of promiscuity is the absence of emotional attachment. Individuals who engage in promiscuous behavior may separate sex from emotions, placing less emphasis on developing emotional intimacy with their partners. This can lead to engaging in sexual activities without requiring a deeper connection or emotional involvement.

Promiscuous individuals often engage in frequent partner changes. They may actively seek new sexual partners, desiring novelty or variety in their sexual experiences. This can result in a higher turnover of partners, as individuals constantly seek out new connections without committing to a long-term relationship.

Promiscuity typically involves a diminished focus on emotional intimacy. Individuals who engage in promiscuous behavior may prioritize physical pleasure or sexual exploration over establishing a deep emotional connection. They may avoid opening up emotionally or sharing personal feelings with their sexual partners, instead focusing solely on the physical aspects of the relationship.

A common characteristic of promiscuity is the indiscriminate selection of sexual partners. Promiscuous individuals may not have strict criteria or preferences when selecting their sexual partners. They may engage with individuals of various backgrounds, ages, or relationship statuses without considering long-term or emotional compatibility factors.

Promiscuity can involve a disregard for potential consequences. Those who engage in promiscuous behavior may not fully consider the physical, emotional, or social consequences of their actions. They may engage in risky sexual behaviors without taking necessary precautions or considering the potential impact on their health or relationships.

ALTERNATIVE RELATIONSHIPS

I became deeply involved in the LGBTQ community. No, not everyone who is same-sex attracted has experienced sexual abuse. Still, there is a population within the LGBTQ community where this is a common story or theme, as they have a history of experiencing some form of sexual abuse.

After experiencing sexual abuse, some may choose to date people of the same sex as a way to regain control over their lives. It can be a way for survivors to regain a sense of control and autonomy, allowing them to make choices that align with their desires and comfort levels. Same-sex dating may feel safer because it enables them to form relationships built on trust and mutual understanding, without the power imbalances and societal expectations often present in heterosexual relationships.

For survivors who struggle with trust issues, dating someone of the same sex can provide a safe environment where they feel more secure and can work on rebuilding trust. It can also serve as a means for survivors to explore and embrace themselves, as they navigate self-discovery and personal development. Additionally, engaging in same-sex dating can create a support network of individuals who have experienced similar struggles, offering empathy and understanding. There is a lot of support offered in the LGBTQ+ community, that you may not see in any other community.

I once had someone ask me, "What do you see in women?" For me, women were a source of safety. I had struggled for quite some time, unsure of my preference between dating men and women, until I finally decided to exclusively date women. That's where I was, and that's where I stayed for the majority of my life. It's been almost ten years since I left that lifestyle, and I would tell anyone that it was something that only God could have done.

This chapter has illuminated the complex ways in which trauma can impact approaches to intimacy and relationships. This can result in emotional barriers, physical discomfort, and difficulties with trust. We have explored various coping mechanisms, including same-sex relationships, as survivors seek to regain control and understanding in their lives.

Remember that healing is a journey, and seeking professional guidance and relying on God's grace can be pivotal in overcoming the impact of trauma on intimacy. As we navigate these challenges, may we find comfort in knowing that God is close to the brokenhearted, offering solace and restoration to those who seek His healing touch (Psalm 34:18, NIV). In Him, there is hope for transformation and a path to fulfilling, loving connections.

" A man's heart plans his way, But the Lord directs his steps." - Proverbs 16:9 NKJV

Church and Intimacy

*Now the Spirit expressly says that in latter times some
will depart from the faith, giving heed to deceiving
spirits and doctrines of demons..." -1 Timothy
1:4 NKJV*

In my days of being spiritual but not religious (SBNR) and
agnostic, I had the opportunity to meet people from various
backgrounds who had abandoned organized religion or
become disillusioned with the Church.

This is one of those topics that is gaining popularity as
people boast about their deconstruction journeys and depart
from their religious communities to seek a different experience
of God. I acknowledge that this issue affects various groups of
people, but I will specifically address the impact of sexual
assault on the relationship between believers and the Church,
as well as the necessity for an appropriate response from the
church to address this escalating problem.

I know someone who was molested as a child. They were
once pagan but eventually returned to Christianity, where

they now serve as a pastor. This man married another man as soon as same-sex marriage was legalized in the country.

He and a group of boys were sexually abused in church when he was younger. The issue came to light and the parents were informed about what happened to the boys. However, all parents decided to let the church handle the situation through church discipline instead of involving the local police.

The boys were minors and had no say in their parents' decisions, but their families all seemed to be on the same page about not embarrassing themselves or bringing shame to the house of God. The minister stepped down for a year and underwent church counseling. After being cleared by church administration and completing all the necessary requirements for reinstatement, he was allowed to return to his position within a year. The boys never received the help and counseling they needed. Instead, the focus was on protecting the reputation of the church and their parents, rather than providing proper care for them.

By the time they reached an age to make life decisions for themselves, most of the boys walked away not only from the church but also from God. They all identified as either bisexual or gay men, with one individual going even further and starting the process of transitioning to become a woman.

The pastor eventually went to seminary, where he began studying the Bible, and later became the pastor of his own church. He believed that God had called him to ministry, so he established an inclusive church where the LGBTQ+ community could find acceptance and belonging.

He preached against many of the things that most churches preached, and his agenda became increasingly evident; he had waged war against the body of Christ. He would preach, sometimes to the point where his anger towards the church would manifest so strongly in his sermons that even the members who were advocates for inclusivity sensed that something was amiss.

Not every assault victim has an issue with the church, unlike this pastor. However, some assault victims, to a degree, have an issue with the church concerning their assault because they believe the church failed to meet their expectations in addressing the issue. They had a need that was not fulfilled. So, instead of seeking healing, they revolt against the institutions and become heretical or apostates.

These individuals truly need to experience the love of God. The body of Christ has become accustomed to people using "church hurt" as a default excuse for not attending church. As a result, we have mistakenly grouped everyone together, even though not all experiences of church hurt are the same.

A person who has experienced sexual abuse within the church or by someone claiming to represent the church suffers from a much deeper level of pain than someone who has merely had their ego bruised. We have to keep this in mind when making coy comments like the one I read the other day that said, "People hurt you, not the church; that's just an excuse not to go to church." There were so many "amens" on the comment thread, and I remember thinking, "Where is the love in such a post?"

If a woman finds herself in a domestic violence situation, most churchgoers will advise her to leave and seek safety. For a trauma victim, the church can trigger the same panic. So, people may flee in order to seek safety. But as believers, we have to love like Christ in order to start dismantling the walls that afflict others.

As a counselor within a law enforcement agency, I often encountered individuals who were reluctant to work with me solely because of my profession in law enforcement. I had the position to wield authority, but I would hear them out and listen to their apprehensions. I discovered one simple tactic that never fails to win anyone over. I learned to apologize on behalf of the institution.

No, I had nothing to do with their past experiences with law enforcement officers. But I validated their feelings and apologized on behalf of the institution. As an employee, I represented the institution. So, the fact that someone acknowledged their pain, representing the institution, broke down barriers.

I would then use that as leverage during group discussions to educate others about my job and the significance of my role. I also used that time to explain the role of the officer and the supervisor in the office, emphasizing how we were there to assist them. As colleagues, we frequently interacted, respected each other's expertise, and were aligned in our mission.

I believe that moving forward, many churches that have not received this revelation will have to. Not everyone is against the church. Their experiences and trauma have convinced them that the church cannot help them and is not the sanctuary they believed it to be. But even the patient bears responsibility in finding the right place for themselves to obtain what they need. For believers, having a relationship with a local community of believers is crucial.

Before meeting my pastors, it was almost impossible for me to find loving and compassionate leaders. I've finally been blessed in that aspect, and for that I'm grateful, but it took almost two decades to get here. I would encourage everyone to pursue and find the place that can help them. Not just a place that agrees with you, but a place that embodies the heart of Christ to assist you in repairing and healing the brokenness that has caused a separation between you and the church.

BONUS: Broken Relationship With the Church

~~~

TRIGGER WARNING

When we think of sexual assault victims, the common perception often leans toward women. However, the shoes of Tamar can be worn by individuals of any gender.

I openly share and speak about my life within the LGBTQ community because I have encountered many people, formed numerous friendships, and listened to countless stories of people within this community, which I was once a part of, share similar experiences. Some of their stories were deeply disturbing. Let me share one such story.

For the purpose of this narrative, I'll refer to him as Tamir instead of Tamar. Tamir was a remarkable individual; he would readily give you the shirt off his back. Singing and worshiping were his passions, and he seized every opportunity to raise his voice in praise. His love for the Lord and people was evident, yet he deliberately avoided setting foot inside a church.

Initially, I thought Tamir's reluctance towards church might stem from his effeminate nature, perhaps due to his desire to avoid sermons condemning his lifestyle. However, the truth was much more chilling. Tamir's aversion to church was driven by paralyzing panic attacks and rage that struck every time he attempted to attend a service.

Tamir's connection to church stretched back to his childhood. He was the lead singer in the children's choir and displayed talent in both singing and playing various instruments. His commitment was unwavering, often being the first to arrive and the last to leave choir practice. Even his single mother, despite her busy life, ensured that he was part of the church community.

The choir director eventually stepped in to help make sure that Tamir arrived at all the practices, and took him home afterward. The insidious grooming process began during these rides. The ride became a breeding ground for conversation and manipulation – a touch here, a suggestive comment there, a mix of encouragement and inappropriate advances.

As choir practice sessions extended, Tamir found solace in the additional time spent learning music on the keyboard. The director, who was 26 at the time, became a father figure to the impressionable 12-year-old Tamir. However, the nature of their relationship took a dark turn when Tamir was around 13.

It was at this point that the choir director introduced Tamir to the world of sex and pornography. What followed was a prolonged period (years) of manipulation and exploitation, leaving Tamir emotionally entangled with his abuser. The relationship had gone on for so long that Tamir believed that the director loved him and that they would be together. He looked forward to turning 18 because he would legally be able to marry the youth minister. By the time he turned 17, the director had lost interest in him. It wasn't long before Tamir noticed that the director had begun grooming another boy, echoing the age when the 'relationship' initially began with Tamir.

This rejection left Tamir devastated. His mental health deteriorated, and he realized the painful reality of his situation – he had been groomed, taken advantage of, and misled to believe it was a relationship. He had inadvertently interpreted his own rape as a twisted form of love. By the time this truth emerged, his formative years had been marred by a disturbing relationship with a grown man.

Years later, it came to light that the same man had victimized many other boys. Astonishingly, the abuser was still playing a significant role within churches – he had become a worship pastor. The church seemed more concerned about preserving the reputation of a 'man of God' than acknowledging the numerous lives he had irreparably damaged.

Tamir's journey through adulthood was marked by battles with depression, leading him in and out of psychiatric facilities. He sought solace and love in the arms of various men, driven by the misguided belief that these connections could recreate the distorted sense of love and affection he experienced as a young victim at the hands of the choir director.

For Tamir, returning to church was out of the question.

He said he'd never go to church because he refused to be condemned by the same place that made him who he was.

Part Three

~~~

SPIRITUAL EFFECTS

What are Spiritual Effects?

When we examine the spiritual consequences of sexual trauma, we are delving into the essence of one's faith. It is a place where it seems as though a fragment of your soul, which once sought comfort, optimism, and guidance through your connection with God, has been shattered and lost amidst overwhelming emotions.

One consequence of this spiritual upheaval is the loss of trust in God. Doubts arise, questioning how a benevolent God could allow such a heinous act. Asking questions such as, "Where was God when I needed Him the most?" can make it challenging to maintain belief in a God who seems to have abandoned or disappointed you during your most difficult moments.

Spirituality often provides comfort, guidance, and purpose for many people. It provides a framework for navigating life's challenges, finding resilience in difficult times, and exploring our own selves and the world around us. Spiritual transformations empower us to navigate adversity, find meaning in our experiences, and cultivate contentment.

Sexual trauma can blind us to the benefits of spirituality

by severing our connection with our purpose, leaving us adrift without our inner compass. It can diminish our self-esteem and confidence, weaken our self-reliance, confuse our sense of self, create resentment, and even result in spiritual disillusionment. This disillusionment can destroy our perception of God.

It is important to acknowledge the influence of sexual trauma on our spirituality and our search for meaning in life. We must also recognize the impact of sexual trauma on our spiritual well-being by examining how it has affected us. The upcoming chapters will explore these aspects, providing valuable insights and guidance on how to address these impacts on our journey toward healing.

Challenge of Forgiveness

Forgiveness is frequently misunderstood.

> "Then Peter came to Him and said, "Lord, how often shall my brother sin against me, and I forgive him? Up to seven times?" Jesus said to him, "I do not say to you, up to seven times, but up to seventy times seven." -Matthew 18:21-22 NKJV

Can you imagine having to forgive someone 490 times (seventy times seven), especially for the same offense? Jesus was essentially teaching us the importance of forgiveness and the challenge it can be for many people. Some individuals have a knack for provoking us, pushing our buttons, and causing offense. Despite this, we are advised to forgive them.

As a counselor, I can attest that when working with individuals who feel stuck in life, there is often an underlying issue of unforgiveness. Once we address the root of the issue, clients often express sentiments such as, "They don't deserve my forgiveness" or "I can forgive them if they apologize." I then pose the question, "What if they never apologize?" Should you continue to suffer and be consumed by offense because they refuse to apologize? In my experience, it is difficult for people to admit to the harm they've caused. The more egregious the wrongdoing, the less likely someone is to admit their fault, resulting in a lower chance of receiving an apology. Sometimes, they may deny their actions and accuse you of lying.

In many cases, if we base our decision solely on what was done to us, we would have a strong argument for not forgiving someone. Although in some cases it's arguably justified, holding onto unforgiveness is detrimental to both emotional and spiritual well-being. Forgiveness is not dependent on the actions of the person who hurt or offended you; they may or may not take responsibility for their actions. Forgiveness is essential for your sanity, peace of mind, and your relationship with God. I once met someone who was angry with God because they believed that a God, who would expect them to forgive someone as vile as their perpetrator, was disconnected from the reality of being human and did not deserve to be called God.

I believe that God is deeply connected to His creation and understands the human condition, which is why He emphasizes the importance of forgiveness. He knows that He did not create us to bear such burdens, and He understands the consequences of them.

We are currently selling our home and preparing to move. I went to the store to get a cart for transporting boxes. The available equipment included a hand truck dolly with a 600 lb capacity and a flatbed cart with a 300 lb capacity. I paused in the store and decided to call my husband for advice on which one to choose. I assumed that the 600 lb cart would be the better buy because it could hold more weight, even though the 300 lb cart is user-friendly and reduces the risk of injury.

I sent the pictures and specifications to my husband, who instructed me to get the 300 lb cart. I told him that it carried less weight compared to the others. He responded, "I won't be carrying anything over 300 lbs." Movers have specialized equipment to handle excessive weight, and my husband understood his own limits.

Unforgiveness is something that exceeds our emotional and spiritual limits. Unforgiveness can have a destructive impact on people's lives as we often try to bear burdens that we are not equipped to handle, leading to harm to ourselves. My husband recognized the wisdom in hiring professional movers who have the necessary equipment to lift heavy objects that he couldn't handle himself. Learning to forgive allows us to release the burden and give it to God, who has the ability to handle what could otherwise be destructive. Forgiveness is about discerning what to hold onto and what to let go, allowing oneself to move forward.

Forgiving someone does not imply absolving them or allowing them to "win." It also does not mean that their actions will go unaddressed. Rather, it means that you are not the one who determines how their actions will be addressed.

> "Beloved, do not avenge yourselves, but rather give
> place to wrath; for it is written, "Vengeance is
> Mine, I will repay," says the Lord." - Romans
> 12:19 NKJV

I understand that it can be difficult because we often want to seek revenge ourselves and say, "See, that's what you deserve!" There is a part of us that wants to take pleasure in being proven right, especially when someone has wronged us. It is satisfying to witness life serving them their deserved punishment of revenge and vindication. These thoughts contradict scripture and go against the heart that God desires for us to have. Even in our suffering and in the actions of others against us, God uses these situations to help us grow and become better versions of ourselves.

> "43 "You have heard that it was said, 'You shall love your neighbor and hate your enemy.' 44 But I say to you, love your enemies, bless those who curse you, do good to those who hate you, and pray for those who spitefully use you and persecute you, 45 that you may be sons of your Father in heaven; for He makes His sun rise on the evil and on the good, and sends rain on the just and on the unjust. 46 For if you love those who love you, what reward have you? Do not even the tax collectors do the same? 47 And if you greet your brethren only, what do you do more than others? Do not even the tax collectors do so? 48 Therefore you shall be perfect, just as your Father in heaven is perfect." - Matthew 5:43-48 NKJV

Forgiveness goes beyond our natural inclinations. It requires us to release the weight of holding onto grudges and have faith in God's fairness and wisdom. As we practice forgiveness, we release the burdens that weigh us down emotionally and spiritually, enabling God to carry the load that was never meant for us to bear. However, the process of forgiveness can be challenging, and doubts may arise during the journey.

Forgiveness is important. Jesus's teaching of forgiving seventy times seven emphasizes the importance of quick forgiveness, not only for the benefit of our peace and spiritual well-being. Unforgiveness burdens us, while forgiveness is a wise act that transfers that burden to God. Trusting in God's plan does not mean giving up on justice. It means finding emotional and spiritual liberation, even in the face of frustration.

"And whenever you stand praying, if you have anything against anyone, forgive him, that your Father in heaven may also forgive you your trespasses. But if you do not forgive, neither will your Father in heaven forgive your trespasses." -Mark 11:25-26 NKJV

Finding Freedom From Bondage

Psychology teaches us that trauma can have a lasting impact on our bodies and minds. It has a tendency to linger and attach itself to us. Our bodies hold onto the memory of pain, even when we attempt to forget or move on mentally. These memories create spiritual strongholds within our souls, which are deeply ingrained beliefs and thought patterns that bind us and influence our thoughts, emotions, and actions.

Trauma hinders our ability to fully embrace life, acting as a form of bondage that keeps us tied to past pain.

I have encountered individuals with incredible talents and potential who have become trapped in situations such as repeated incarcerations or addiction. It is clear that no amount of success or external achievements can heal their souls.

In "Battles and Trials: A Fight for Deliverance" I tell the story of an institutionalized inmate. The prison had become his home, offering acceptance and a sense of belonging that he couldn't find in the outside world. He had adjusted to his circumstances, but he still couldn't achieve true healing and freedom. To him, his fellow inmates were like family, more so than anyone he had ever known outside of prison.

This teaches us a valuable lesson. Sometimes, we become so accustomed to pain and challenging circumstances that we start to see them as normal and accept them as a natural part of our lives. We often settle for less because we acknowledge that things could be worse, even if the place we end up in is a prison cell. God desires for us to be free in Him.

In order to break free from bondage, we must first recognize its existence and identify the patterns it has created in our lives. We must acknowledge this in order to heal because it takes courage to confront pain. Healing the soul is a journey that requires time, patience, and self-compassion. It involves uncovering layers of trauma and replacing falsehoods with the truth of God.

2 Corinthians 10:4 reminds us that

"The weapons of our warfare are not of the flesh but
    have divine power to destroy strongholds."

We can free ourselves from the limitations that hold us back by praying, seeking God's guidance, undergoing therapy, and renewing our minds with His Word.

"Jesus answered them, 'Most assuredly, I say to you,
    whoever commits sin is a slave of sin.' And a slave
    does not abide in the house forever, but a son
    abides forever. Therefore, if the Son makes you
    free, you shall be free indeed." -John 8:34-36
    NKJV.

John 8:36 declares that freedom comes from Jesus Christ. How often do we become enslaved by our experiences? Strongholds must be released or eradicated from the soul in order to break their grip on our lives and prevent them from manipulating our perceptions. While there are numerous solutions and alternatives available in the world, it is important to recognize that whatever the world has to offer is only a temporary fix. True freedom can only be found in Christ Jesus.

Some individuals claim to be Christians and profess belief in Christ, yet they have never sought Him for deliverance from the weight of their past. It seems that they believe God can do almost anything, except heal their minds and hearts from their past traumas. The need for healing becomes a hindrance in all aspects of their lives, and some are unaware that many of their failures stem from it.

I have heard some believers say that they feel stagnant, unaware that the impact of trauma has hindered their advancement. It's as if they are unable to fulfill their purpose and progress in what God has intended for them in this lifetime. They experience doubt, chronic cycles of failure, incomplete projects, lack of motivation, low self-esteem, lack of consistency, and instability, all of which stem from a need to break free.

Spiritual strongholds keep us limited.

Jesus Christ has the power to free us from the weight of our past and guide us toward a life filled with purpose and fulfillment. It is crucial to seek healing from Him for our mindset and heart, as trauma, if left unchecked, can destroy us.

God does not want us to live in bondage, and He provides a way to find healing and freedom. By seeking His guidance, we can shatter the strongholds that have kept us captive. His healing can free us from the hold of our past and empower us to fulfill our purpose and potential.

"Now the Lord is the Spirit; and where the Spirit of the Lord *is*, there *is* liberty. " - 2 Corinthians 3-17 NKJV

Faith after Trauma

Have you ever considered how trauma affects our faith? When we experience trauma, it can shake the foundation of our beliefs, causing us to feel torn between faith and skepticism.

I don't believe that losing faith is something anyone intentionally sets out to do. Sometimes, the pain we endure can be so overwhelming that our faith no longer appears to satisfy the voids within us. Sexual trauma is an area that the church has often struggled to address openly, leaving many children and adults suffering in silence. This struggle has allowed the enemy to manipulate the minds of survivors, convincing them that the church is indifferent to their situations and that God has forsaken them.

In an ideal world, every church would have staff members who are trained in trauma-informed care, but that's not realistic. In many cases, it is advisable for a church that lacks the necessary resources to address this issue to refrain from attempting to provide services that it cannot sustain, as it may result in more harm than good. It should also be considered that if you have the opportunity to seek Christian and Biblical counseling, you should understand that these may not follow the typical style of therapy provided by a mental health professional. This type of setting may be acceptable for some individuals, but depending on the severity of your situation, you may require both professional and spiritual counseling, if it is accessible.

Our beliefs and expectations about faith, its purpose, and how it should benefit us ultimately determine whether someone becomes closer or further away during challenging times. It seems that as soon as we decide to drift away from God, there is always a false belief system or some other vice waiting to pull us even further away from Him.

> "But without faith, it is impossible to please Him, for he who comes to God must believe that He is, and that He is a rewarder of those who diligently seek Him." - Hebrews 11:6 NKJV

The enemy's assignment is to deceive and take on any form necessary to make us doubt that Christ is the answer. The enemy capitalized on my ignorance as a youth, taking advantage of my lack of discernment, as well as my hurt and anger, to make me question the existence of God. The enemy used all those things to drive a wedge between God and me, essentially creating a division between my purpose and destiny in God.

When I started studying the Bible, I came across Hebrews 11:6, which states, "Without faith, it is IMPOSSIBLE to please Him." I realized that the strategies the enemy employs to distance us from God and attack our belief and faith actually put us in a position where we cannot please God. Our lack of faith and belief in the face of challenging circumstances and the skepticism that arises puts us in an unfavorable position with God, and the enemy is well aware of this. Many people cannot realize their purpose in God because the enemy has distorted their perception of God. Abuse resulting in trauma that affects one's faith is a tormenting experience.

I remember a few months before surrendering my life to Christ, I had a dream where I found myself standing in the middle of a graveyard. It was pouring rain, and I found myself digging a grave alongside a mysterious creature. I remember not wanting to dig the grave, but I had no control over my actions. In the dream, I had the opportunity to see inside a hub station where another creature was using an electronic touch-screen monitor.

Whatever action this creature selected was the action I would do. I remember having the opportunity to glance at the headstones, and to my surprise, my name was engraved on one of them. Whatever creature was controlling me had me digging my own grave. Then the creature selected a weapon, and I was expected to pick it up, inflict harm upon myself, and fall into the grave. I woke up in terror because the dream felt so real.

It wasn't until after I had given my life to Christ that I realized the depths of my alignment with the enemy. The enemy was revealing his intentions for my life, and for many years, I had believed the lie. I had convinced myself that life without God was fine and that I didn't need Him as much as I actually did. I grew up in church, so it wasn't as if I didn't know God. It was the hurt and then the hatred that drew me so far away from God. The longer you live detached from God, the harder it becomes to recognize God's relevance in your life, and the greater the likelihood that you will never experience the peace and healing you desire.

There's a gospel song called "Nobody Greater" by artist Vashawn Mitchell. I believe this perfectly describes the journey that people take away from God, only to return and realize that He was all they ever needed from the start. Trauma can drive people to search for something unknown, all around the world, only to find themselves unfulfilled by any of it.

In conclusion, trauma can have a profound impact on our faith, creating a divide between our beliefs and the painful experiences we go through. It's not a deliberate loss of faith, but rather a consequence of the immense pain that can make our faith feel inadequate to heal our deepest wounds. Personal experiences, such as vivid dreams, can sometimes reflect the enemy's intention to lead us astray from God. However, it is crucial to recognize these deceptions and instead turn to our faith, which holds the true answers to our healing and fulfillment. As the gospel song "Nobody Greater" reminds us, the quest for satisfaction outside of God can never match the wholeness discovered in Him, particularly when confronted with the challenges of trauma.

"And do not be conformed to this world, but be transformed by the renewing of your mind, that you may prove what *is* that good and acceptable and perfect will of God." -Romans 12:2 NKJV

Unveiling Identity

As we near the end of this book, I would like to provide a word on identity. As believers, we cannot be ignorant of the devices of the enemy, and trauma is one of those devices. Trauma has the power to shape our perception of ourselves, others, and even our beliefs about God. Trauma, if given the power, has the ability to completely remove us from our relationship with God and cause us to abandon our destiny in God.

I came to understand that the trauma I experienced was not just a random event, but rather a deliberate effort and a demonic assignment to hinder me from ever realizing why God created me. We were all created for a specific purpose, and the enemy tried to make me resent God, hoping that it would cause me to reject my true identity. Unfortunately, I fell into this trap for a long time. The assignment of sexual trauma is particularly damaging because it manipulates you into straying from your intended path.

I have witnessed numerous people who were blessed with spiritual gifts such as prophecy, worship, evangelism, artistry, teaching, and more. However, they have made the decision to turn away from their divine calling and separate themselves from God. They blamed God for something that God never desired to happen, but rather, it was a result of sin. They hold deep resentment and disdain towards anything related to Christ. The enemy's plan is to keep them in a state of instability, constantly pursuing worldly success and neglecting the true fulfillment that comes from embracing their authentic identity.

Where there is unhealed trauma, deception exists. The enemy manipulates our pain and suffering, leading us to believe that we can find fulfillment and healing outside of God's kingdom.

Unresolved trauma can lead to rebellion against God, and scripture states that rebellion is as the sin of witchcraft (1 Samuel 15:23). However, by seeking healing, discovering our purpose, embracing our identity, and accepting God's restoration, we can overcome the schemes of the enemy.

Remember, your purpose remains intact. God's plans for your life are still intact, waiting to be fully realized. Embrace the healing journey and allow God to restore you from within. As you navigate the complexities of your past, present, and future, remember that you are not alone. God is always by your side, providing love, grace, and guidance.

May this book inspire your healing, remind you of your worth, and encourage you. You are fearfully and wonderfully made, with a unique calling that only you can fulfill. Trust in God's faithfulness, and let His love guide you toward restoration.

"The Spirit Himself bears witness with our spirit that

we are children of God, and if children, then heirs —heirs of God and joint heirs with Christ, if indeed we suffer with Him, that we may also be glorified together." Romans 8:16-17 NKJV

Embracing Radical Self-Care for Lasting Healing

Dear Cherished Reader,

As we come to the end of Tamar's Scars, I want to leave you with a heartfelt call to action. Throughout this book, we have explored the depths of pain, trauma, and healing, and now it's time for application.

Here are some steps you can take as you continue your journey of deliverance, healing, and wholeness:

- **Seek God with all your heart:** Your relationship with God is key to your healing journey. Take time to pray, read His Word, and worship Him. Let Him guide you, comfort you, and reveal His unfailing love to you.
- **Reach out for support**: Remember, you don't have to face this journey alone. Seek out a supportive community that understands and embraces you. It could be a counselor, a support group, or trusted friends and family who will walk with you through the ups and downs.

- **Share your story:** Your story is powerful and can bring hope and healing to others. Don't be afraid to share your experiences, triumphs, and struggles. By doing so, you can inspire and encourage others who may be going through similar challenges.
- **Stay vigilant in your healing**: Healing is a lifelong journey. Be patient with yourself and practice self-care. Keep using the tools and principles you've learned to maintain your emotional, relational, and spiritual well-being. Remember to be kind to yourself and give yourself grace along the way.
- **Build healthy boundaries**: Set clear boundaries in your relationships and prioritize your emotional and mental well-being. Learn to say no to things that drain you and yes to activities that nurture and uplift you.
- **Embrace self-compassion:** Be kind and gentle with yourself as you navigate the healing process— practice self-compassion by acknowledging your pain, offering yourself forgiveness, and treating yourself with love and understanding.
- **Foster a support network**: Surround yourself with people who uplift, encourage, and support you on your healing journey. Seek out individuals who understand your experiences and can provide a safe space for you to share and grow. Nurture meaningful connections that contribute to your healing and growth. But most of all, connect with intercessors who can intercede for you, pick you up in the spirit, and know to pray.

As you take these steps, always remember that you are not alone. God is right beside you, guiding your steps and pouring out His love upon you. You are a cherished child of God, and your healing journey is a testament to His amazing grace and transformative power.

May you experience the peace, hope, and strength that come from our Lord and Savior, Jesus Christ. May your story of healing be a beacon of light for others, leading them to find their own paths to wholeness and restoration.

With love and blessings,

Author of Tamar's Scars

About the Author

Renikko Bivens is a talented author, counselor, and Bible teacher committed to helping others on their personal journeys. With extensive experience in criminal justice and counseling, she brings a wealth of knowledge to support others in their healing and transformation.

She holds an MA in Organizational Management, a BA in Social and Criminal Justice, and an AA in Ecclesiastical Theological Studies. She is also a CADC-II and ICADC, which provides her with a comprehensive understanding of human behavior, justice, and spirituality.

She combines her understanding of Scripture with the leading of the Holy Spirit, offering timely guidance and inspiration. As the founder of Graced to Write LLC and The Spirit-Led Pen Blog, she creates impactful literary works that uplift readers through her writing. Renikko's compassionate counseling approach has positively impacted lives by helping people discover healing and freedom.

Outside of her professional life, Renikko finds joy in her family and actively serves in her local church. Rooted in her upbringing in Central Georgia, she is committed to making a positive impact in her community. She strives to empower others to embrace their God-given purpose and experience transformation in all aspects of their lives.

Also by Renikko Bivens

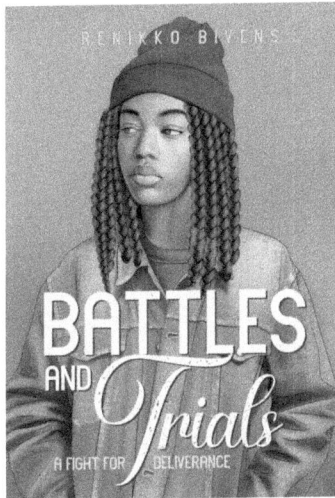

Battles & Trials: A Fight For Deliverance

www.ingramcontent.com/pod-product-compliance
Lightning Source LLC
LaVergne TN
LVHW051421080426
835508LV00022B/3181